ORIGINAL POEMS

By Ursula Dehne

July 2009

Ursula Hanners is now Ursula Dehne and lives with her new German husband in Northumberland, NH in a beautiful chalet on the Amanoosuc River. The surroundings inspire more of her poetry.

Copyright © Ursula Dehne

All rights reserved
Printed in the United States of America

LIBRARY OF CONGRESS
CATALOG-IN-PUBLICATION DATA

Dehne, Ursula

ISBN 9781936711642

10 9 8 7 6 5 4 3 2 1

Railroad Street Press
394 Railroad Street
Suite 2
St. Johnsbury, VT 05819

Table of Contents

April

May

July

Morning Dew

September

October

November

Music

The Diet

Chris

First Fallen Snow

Basketball

Table of Contents

Dry Snow

Moose, Moose, Moose

Katherine

Opera

It's Getting Cold

Warm Wishes

John

911

Why Worry

Lilly

December 24/18

April

Cool is the air,
Patches of snow here and there,
It smells like spring,
So fresh and clean.
A little bit of green,
Can be seen.
It won't be long now
Before it is here.
The month of May
And I will cheer.

MAY

It is May.

It is May, my favorite month.

The air smells fresh and has the taste of spring.

It is the birth of a new season.

Light green can be seen across the mountains.

The grass is growing, the brooks are flowing.

My favorite month is May!!!!!

July

Birdfeeders on the ground.
Sunflower seeds are scattered about.
What could it be?
We set a <u>Have a Heart Trap</u>.
We will find out soon.
Guess what?
It was a big fat raccoon!!!!!

Morning Dew

Morning dew and spiderwebs

So beautiful and delicate

A spiderweb covered with morning dew,

Even Grandmas finest crochet could not match this beauty.

Milkweed so puffy they are ready to burst.

The silky white seedlings soon will emerge.

SEPTEMBER

Mist is rising from the valley.
The valley is still so green and fresh.
As I look to the hills above me.
Leaves are coloring.
Orange
Yellow
and
Red

October

Snowy lace covered mountains above.
Yellow leafy trees below.
A breeze is blowing brisk and cold.
Soon there will be
SNOW
SNOW
SNOW

NOVEMBER

Warm oatmeal still between my teeth.

While crunchy snow under my feet.

A cold north wind is blowing my way, as I am walking my path today.

This is the season's first snow and in five weeks we will say

Ho, Ho, Ho!

Music

My grandson, Jonathan,
Plays the cello.
To listen to his music
Makes me feel quite mellow.
Tunes were
Nutcracker March, Cats, and
German Waltzing.
It is very exciting.
and I hope he does
lots more
reciting..

The Diet

White fluffy clouds are in the sky.
Look like meringue on a pie.
I wish they were down here.
So I could nibble on them
With a cheer!

Chris

My other grandson, Chris,
Is only fifteen.

You won't believe what I have seen.

In the <u>Music Man, he played</u>
Professor Hill.

I flew to Oklahoma to see the performance

And it was a real thrill!

First Fallen Snow

Fresh fallen snow on my
Walking path.
So clean and white.
It's shining like crystals and diamonds
so bright.
What a wonderful day,
So peaceful.
As I am walking,
not even the dogs are barking.

BASKETBALL

"Hey, John, Why do like basketball so much?"

"Basketball is lots of fun!, said John,

"And it's boy stuff (usually)."

"That's sexist," says Katherine, "Girls play too."

"How do you know?" John questions, "I think it's mostly for boys."

"It doesn't mean it's a boy's sport," Katherine replies, There are lots of girls who play basketball really well, like Morriah!"

Maybe I could play against her some day", John says.

"I'm really, really good at getting the ball away from other people...

And I can dribble for nine seconds and shoot the ball at the last second!

I'm really good at making baskets!

Basketball is fun!

I hope I get to play with Morriah

Someday

And win!"

Dry Snow

She says, "Let's make a snowman."
I say, "No, The snow is dry."
She asks, "Why?"
She says, "I thought snow was wet."
I say, "You bet.
To build a snowman
you need wet snow.
This snow fell when it was very cold
And therefore it just won't hold.
As soon as we get a good snow
That's wet,
We will make a snowman
You bet!"

MOOSE, MOOSE, MOOSE

Watch out for the moose!
It is not a goose.
The moose will run
alongside the road,
And then cross over,
If you hit a moose,
You lose.

Katherine

A little girl so beautiful and bright.
She could play, sing, and
dance all night.
This week Christmas bells
were ringing,
And this little girl was singing.
She sang all by herself
so loud and clear,
<u>Ihr Kinderlein kommet</u>,
On stage she stood
And got a big cheer.

OPERA

Christopher now 28 singing
And performing in operas across
the country and Europe.
Some of his performances have been
The Marriage of Figaro
La boheime
Dau Giovanni
Die Zauber flote
I am very proud of him.
I wish him lots more performances.

It's Getting Cold

The mountains and hillsides
look cold and bare.
There are no leaves anywhere.
Snuggled inside the house are
Dogs and kittens.
Pretty soon we will wear our wool mittens.

Warm Wishes

Purple mittens are knitted by hand.
Nice and warm to give to a friend.
Today is her birthday,
Decemer 5th.
I thought this would make a
Nice little gift.

John

A little boy who just turned four.
When we play we have fun galore.
He is very kind and very sweet.
And he loves chocolates to eat.
Today's his birthday and we celebrate.
And guess what?
There was a big chocolate cake we ate.

911

Once there were two.
Now there are none.
It is so sad that they are gone.
It's not the same without them there.
It has changed lives everywhere.
I wish there was more **love**
In this world.

Why Worry

Heaven above, earth below.
Who will know wherever we go?

This is a question we will all ask.
But, if you believe, it won't be a task.

Your soul goes above and your body below.
This is the way it will always go.

So believe in the Lord
He will take care of you.

Don't worry. Why worry?
He knows what to do.

Lilly

*The sweetest pet I ever had
she even comes up and sleeps
at night on my bed. At 6:00am
she comes up and lays next to
my head, to tell me it's time
to get out of bed.
She has to be wherever I am
She follows me around wherever I go.
She also likes to play in the Snow????
She goes out in the Barn when
I bring in the wood and I know
she would help me, if she could.*

If you have a dream
Inside your heart, don't ever
Let it go, because dreams
Can be the tiny seed
from which tomorrow grows.

December 24/18

*Oh my, oh my 3 years
Have gone by, in sickness
And in health but we
have our wealth, and we
are happy in our new home
on the river you look at
the ice and it gives you
a shiver. But we are cozy
and warm and it won't do
us any harm.*

LOVE

What would be like
If winter without snow
And weeks without sunshine
And summer without flowers.
And live without love.

Love puts the music in laughter
The beauty in song

The warmth on a shoulder
The gentle in strong?????
Love puts the magic in memories
The sunshine in skies
The gladness in giving
The starlight in eyes.
Love puts the fun in together
The sad in apart.

The hope in tomorrow,
the joy in the heart.

www.ingramcontent.com/pod-product-compliance
Lightning Source LLC
Chambersburg PA
CBHW050816090426
42736CB00021B/3467